Clipping the Wings of Chronos

A Book of Poetry
by

R. T. Sedgwick

A Word with You Press®
Editors and Advocates of Fine Stories in the Digital Age
Moscow, Idaho

Clipping the Wings of Chronos
is published by:
A Word with You Press®

310 East A Street, Suite B, Moscow, Idaho 83843

For information, please direct emails to:
info@awordwithyoupress.com or visit our website:
www.awordwithyoupress.com

Cover design and interior layout: Teri Rider, www.teririder.com
Cover photo by Jim Sedgwick

First Edition
Printed in the United States of America

10 9 8 7 6 5 4 3 2 1   19 20 21 22 23 24 25 26

Clipping the Wings of Chronos

If I had the wings
  of an eagle
    a hummingbird
      or even a butterfly

  and you had the space
    of one afternoon

I'd fly to you
  and we'd find a way
    to clip the wings
      of Chronos

Contents

Clipping the Wings of Chronos

Poetry

Look at its art
        hear its music
                touch its texture
       savor its aroma
              taste its flavor
follow its veins
        of discovery
             of epiphany
       as you excavate
            the mines of white-space

The fresh air *between* raindrops
    the singing *behind* the curtain
        the smoothness *before* you hold her hand
    the open oven *after* removing the bread
the sip of brandy *as* you swallow

Let your river of rain
        arrive at its delta
            let it evaporate
       head back
           to its home in the sky

Yesterday's Meadow Grass

Come with me beyond
the pasture fence
where uneaten weeds
have been given a chance
to grow and thrive
Let meditation bathe our psyches
in a sea of unfettered sunlight
as we look out
on a rutted country road
and watch sleek black crows
peck at carrion

Feel the sun as it stokes
the blaze of mid-day
and note how leaves dance naked
in sunlight
Glimpse time's treasure
as it dashes madly
from one cloak-and-dagger mystery
to another   unfolding
like a sheared string
of paper dolls

A breeze browses the tall saplings
then ducks through
an oak tree
riling only a few of its leaves
signaling that the deep
blue bowl of summer is about to break
though the grapes are not yet ripe
We have all the necessary time
and air needed to breathe and we sleep
so our counted sheep can feed
on yesterday's meadow grass

Without Love...

the heart can become an empty lot
        watching weeds grow
                older before their time

and life nothing more than the lion's
        long wait for appetite
                to return after the kill

Lavender no longer bends down
        to kiss a rose long overgrown
                with the shrubbery of time

Tangled sheets and tangled dreams
        once beautiful here
                are no longer beautiful there

The viscid barb of Big Bang's single
        arrow seems to be turning
                all living blood to coral

but love with its astronomical powers
        can shatter the cosmos
                of planetary isolation

shimmer like wind chimes within
        the heart to give us music
                from the inside out

So please   lead me to that *Promised Land*
        I've not yet visited   and leave
                a little lipstick on my cheek

Dealing With My Muse

My bones will surely die
    unless I learn to follow
        your sly and wanton ways

So rope me in and tame me
    with words that use the palette
        of seasons to paint my poems

Let the meaning of each moment
    last a lifetime like ancient fossils
        and bones that build history

When words fade like shortened
    shadows   pry open your sacred safe
        of secret language

Linger along the lines with me
    lighten my load so I can run
        free like the summer breeze

Keep me willing to take the litmus
    test of truth to the rose petal edges
        of negative space

Travel the pages with me   leave room
    for mutual rewards   knowing
        that nothing but love propels us

Help me through life's rhythms
    so in the end I'll know
        each grain of sand has been well spent

Path Lined with Red Sumac

Another day begins as morning light
          opens like a dancer's fan
followed by a slow limping
          through a lengthy afternoon

And now that evening is upon us
          stars are beginning to disrobe
one by one   and the sky
          is awash in nakedness

Let us never forget to sing
          those songs of our childhood
when love seemed edible
          and flowed like maple syrup

One can learn a lot from the rising
          and setting sun and maybe fathom
the freely-given wisdom
          of each crashing ocean wave

No need to be anywhere or anybody
          but when lines need to be drawn
know we can never be sure where
          nor when to scrub them away

Be glad the abyss of desire will never
          be filled   Threadbare rugs hide less
than do plush ones and it takes practiced
          hands to thread a needle

I like the way your quiet eyes
          shut out all passive judgement
even when the piano in your own
          parlor needs tuning

All wars   whether with self or others
            are lost   And love is running into a hiker
who knows the trail and is willing to help
            you find that path lined with red sumac

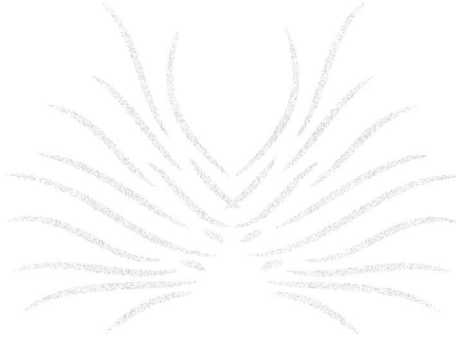

Unfinished Symphony

Everyday un-spools
      like a plush red carpet
awaiting celebrities and trespassers alike

so it was no surprise this morning
      when I woke to the strains
of a song sparrow's unfinished symphony

and when the concert was over
      I stood in unison
with the sun's bravos and friendly ovation

Everything in this world
      is pretty much disguised
as life flips through our unedited manuscripts

I try to keep my wings
      of acceptance unfolded
for any songbird could be a low-flying angel

All critters must fit somewhere
      into this wandering wilderness
like pieces of creation's infinite jigsaw puzzle

Whenever I am forced to wade
      through muddied waters
I let my heart sail high above the muted surface

free to pulse in the wind
      with the assurance of a maestro
who fine-tunes the beat of an entire orchestra

but nothing lasts forever
      and even Schubert sensed
that life itself must end before it's finished

Beginnings
—In the beginning was the Word
John 1:1

What a heroic deed when a blank page
like a silent lake carrying echoes
gives up its pious purity
for the sake of a prolific pen
I'm probably not the only one
in this world whose head
contains such a plethora
of over-sold plot lines
and of course the moon's not to blame
but what about the stars   for it's been said
the entire history of the human race
has been written there
I suppose someday I'll be given
that golden opportunity
to page through God's picture album
and find the answers to such questions
and maybe see my past self
sacrificing another martini
by pouring it over the fresh grave
of an alcoholic friend
Sin certainly has its quirks
If it weren't for the original one
women might have it easier giving birth
and farmers wouldn't be late for supper
From my very beginning
as a humble poet I've learned to worship
the word   truly the root
of all beginnings

No Befores and No Afters

Tall pines bend in the wind
     the way I imagine a hustler
might riffle a stacked deck
        but if there's a message here
           it's been discarded like that
        sudden squadron of geese
rising out of the swamp
     where cattails left behind
kneel beneath budding oaks
        and if there was a messenger
           he won't be saddened for
        nothing's been promised
like the give and take
     of seasons   so there's little
or nothing for him to lose
        Time passes slowly here
           like that carp slugging its way
        through the murky pond
and visitors feel like tourists
     in a foreign land   with little
or no knowledge of customs
        or language   Yet still
           their wounds are easily reopened
        like a vintage book   worn
at the corners pleading
     to be read and re-read
just to make sure they haven't missed
        that misplaced minor chord
           of shame   and there's no way
        for them to rinse off the resulting
lack of self-esteem   Beneath
     the pines stretching far in both
directions   rows of stones
        that once had been strong young
           men and women seem to be at peace
        with no befores and no afters

Artistry of Love

Life's tapestry
       is frequently intertwined
              with fragile threads
unlike the spider's web of carefully crafted dreams

So how are we to navigate
       through stretches mostly filled
              with unfamiliar faces
in a world of wild and unspoken longings

One way is to grasp and hold tightly
       the hands of the clocks
              of our youth
when we skimmed poetry like frost off morning chores

For the poet knows language
       can be a leverage
              to his advantage
and that the force of verbs can set nouns in motion

Just as Vincent Van Gogh knew
       swirl and *stroke* were perfect executors
              for his blurred vision of sky
and would excite our senses in '*Starry Night*'

Some say that even love
       may be an unfinished set
              of streaks and highlights
so I paint your portrait in colors that will not fade

Inner Mountain

There's a wind up here
       so strong and gusty
I lean into it
       to maintain my gait

The trail is steep
       but I somehow know
I must climb all the way
       to the top

No safety lines
       no signposts   nor
evidence of anyone
       here before me

Winding past the tree line
       I view a world receding
almost erased   as I begin
       to uncover the *who* in me

Now at the apex I stand tall
       like a bighorn ram
proud to have climbed
       my inner mountain

In the meadows below
       many are still chewing
over their dreams or
       dreams they might yet have

In Search of Grace

It is the season of wasps being drawn
into the shade of Sugar Plums
Days that once sprawled on my front porch
now scurry out the back door

I sometimes think the world forgets
I'm still around   a mere porch light
forming vain glimpses of temporary glow
that maybe a lowly moth or two might notice

Scale is the only real difference
between us and the birth and death
of stars   so maybe I should survey
the night sky for possible clues

I left my briefcase with all its notes
somewhere deep in my dreams
in search of a woodland stream where
the Spirit of God still hovers over water
I want to forget how you broke bread
as though it were a day-old promise

I don't need to understand everything
all I want is for life to flow like quicksilver
no pauses or slowing down   no more questions
no exclamations   just Grace   unpunctuated

Dandelions

—After reading Pokeberries by Ruth Stone

I started out in small town Indiana
with my grandfather's hollyhocks
and Mom's bed of zinnias   We lived
on fried potatoes and thickened tomatoes
Mom wrung out our sheets by hand
Dad laid brick and trapped muskrats
drank Old Crown beer and played poker
He married Mom after watching her walk
past the pool room in a one-piece bathing suit
They drove off to Brimfield and pledged their vows
before a store-front Justice of the Peace
and someone filled their Model-T up with snow
My whole life has been stained by dandelions
No woman seemed right for me   I was awkward
until Cheryl entered stage left onto my proscenium
I don't think you need to ask what that means
I married her and borrowed the money
to buy our own place in California tucked away
in a canyon just south of the Del Mar racetrack
Cheryl died a few years ago   but I'm sticking here
like the overgrown ivy on our chain-link fence
Nothing I've learned since childhood can shake
my grandfather out of me   or my mom   who didn't
just roast our Sunday chickens   she wrung their necks

Psalm of Laughter and Tears

Come sing the meadows into bloom
and dance with me to the distant
drums of thunder   Our existence
is cupped in fragile hands
on this global grid of place and change
sheltered from the cosmos
by a canvas sky   Should blossoms burst
or strife step in to hijack happiness
and our options recede like winter days
we need to re-think the walls
we've built within   which can heal
or destroy like the ebb and flow
of laughter and tears
Neither of us are archeologists
so why would we want to keep digging
into those fragments of yesterday
Instead   let's heed the wake-up call
stand tall and let our bones resist the winds
like limbs of sturdy oaks
Then   and only then   as we scan
the pages of our once-hectic lives
will we note that the paperweight past
seems to have settled and we can sit back
at each day's finish and enjoy
its shadow-tricks as they welcome us
into that silent space called sleep

Twin Sonnets of Youth and Age

I am far away from those wide meadows
where minds wander high above red clover
and canary grass   like undulating bubbles
too big to understand symmetry   where
cotton candy clouds flex like dinosaurs
and where   with a hint of wind   the drag
and thrust of a homemade kite becomes real

Where   as a child   on summer nights after
fireflies   the porch light flooded center stage
as we developed characters and acted out
melodramas for escaping our pretend personas
But even the air was too impatient to sit still
as un-tethered fantasies drifted out to explore
then sailed back home to a welcoming shore

Older now   I realize we all paint the canvases
of our past using color schemes we can condone
I rarely think of the Milky Way anymore
nor that night is eternal for the sun and stars
Somehow I know this jigsaw puzzle will never
be completed   for there are no border pieces
only myriad shapes of hope and unknowing

All knowledge is pockmarked in varying degrees
and the portrait of humankind itself is ill-resolved
I've been taken prisoner by poetry   The poems
I write are remnants torn from my spool's middle
Life's battle will always be order versus disorder
since death keeps leaving voids we cannot fill
so the choice to find meaning resides in our will

Infusion

When life becomes a collage
        of minute things
and shadows of earlier times
        deepen my room
I take extended walks along
        the wide river
where crickets rub their wings
        in mating ritual

It impels me out of the dark
        involuntary
confinement brought on by cradled
        cell phones
and plastic money   even throws
        away its big iron key

A rhythm of dance is infused
        into my bloodstream
allowing deep-rooted sadness
        to evaporate
through my pores until I view life
        as the flutter
of a silk scarf kissed by gentle
        breezes

The Ocean

Your language
      is one of waves
            of rhythm and breath

I speak of what you awakened within me

gills for breathing
      stabilizing fins
            propelling tail

entanglements with your seaweed forests

tastes of crustaceans
      chewiness of kelp
            flavors of algae

as I swam among your laden banquet tables

It's true I've evolved
      legs for walking
            lungs for breathing

I've risen from your waters to honor land

And yet you've beckoned me
      to your wide sandy shore
            where our environs meet

in hopes I'll not lose track of my heritage

I gather seashells
      pick up driftwood
            find a few beach rocks

souvenirs of a salt that will never lose its savor

Torrey Pines State Park

Here on the high red-clay bluffs
       we came together
to meditate and dangle our tired feet
         high over the restless surf

focus attention
        on the hazy horizon
and the unknowns of our future
        swooping in like seagulls

For much of life is what happens
        in between the things we plan
the froth that bubbles up
        from beneath the wave caps

So lean against my shoulder
        the way wind leans
against the ancient Torrey Pines
        bending them back from the sea

I want to capture that closeness
        if only for a few moments
feel the power of torrential waves
        crashing against solid rock

encouraging us to keep the faith
        and trust our oar-less dreams
to carry us across the treacherous waters
        of our doubts   our sighs

Under the Big Top

A pair of ordinary red-tailed hawks
      tread the thermals lifting
          over the back hill

Hardly more than minnows in an aqua sky
      they swim circles over coral tors
          as if fanning singed tail-feathers

Embers so scorched through with scarlet
      I surmise they share the hubris of Icarus
          but maybe not the wax

They dart toward God's sun then fall away
      a mating performance
          on unseen bungee cords

Their repeated *chwirks* of courtship
      discordant plunks on a banjo
          dangling between earth and sun

God himself may be playing Daedalus
      to these wayward hot coals
          caught in a lofty two-ring circus

Committed

The minute we met
  I knew you'd be the current
that would alter the wind
   the river and even electricity

and though it's been years now
  I know I followed you here
so we could spend our time
   in this magic playground

where the air is cool
  and has a naked smell
and the grass speaks
   in little wet tongues

where the hurryings of morning peak at noon
  then ease slowly into midnight
and free will is choosing the types
   of seeds we sow

and we aren't afraid anymore
  of being rescued
from those hidden plans for us
   yet to be revealed

we simply label our time store it
  and once in a while offer thanks
that our two-person crosscut saw truly enjoys
   its interaction with wood

and this we will continue doing
  until we take our last drink
from the unmarked pitcher that pours out
   our numbered days

The Way You Tilt Your Cheek

As we approach the end
       of another string of empty
afternoons   it's comforting to know our past
       stays close to us

All day I'd been wishing
       I had the power   to poke holes
in the collage-tissued sky   but by dusk it had all
       fermented to buttermilk

Now that evening's almost here   it's beginning
       to seem more inviting
as it sweetens   so tempting   so soluble
       a rare perfume behind the ear

Centuries have been floating leisurely
       through time   like galleons   forever
while the sun works its head off   from dawn to dusk
       never once   seeing a night like this

It used to be easy
       for me to fall asleep
by enumerating sheep   but that quit working long ago
       so many lost ones

But the one thing that moves me   keeps
       me going   is the way you tilt
your cheek in my direction   and to think it only began
       with a casual glance

Unum Diem ad Tempus

Breath and flesh abridge
each night's new dark
as rebirth beckons
from beyond the vestigial

We fling and flourish
one more day
on ad infinitum's path
between abysses

Grace wreaks havoc
on our thick-skinned self
then deflects incoming arrows
of fear and pride

Advancing us another notch
along our ratchet   as we don
knee-pads of gratitude
for faith in The Great Unknown

Living Waters

You've heard it before   that life's a river
wide   narrow   fast   or meandering

some overflowing their banks   others with
ready-to-become arroyo amounts of water

All are driven by their gravitational potential
a yearning to head towards the boundless sea

and though each may look the same today
one can never wade into yesterday's water

There must be a persistent river somewhere
though reduced to a trickle still marches on

and when it comes to where it once flowered
as a waterfall is reduced to individual droplets

yet proudly sends each drop   one at a time
over the cliff and onto the desert floor below

creating an ever growing pool of nourishment
for the local community of flora and fauna

happy in its reflective role for the time being
That's the kind of river I want my life to mirror

The Back-side of Shadow

Each morning
I dive into a pool
not knowing if I can swim

and day begins
like the strumming
of a Gospel guitar

followed by
a promising prayer
from my personal pulpit

Sunlight filters
into the bathroom
through bare-branched trees

My morning reflection
is never the guy
I think he should be

I guess we all choose
our stones for pushing
up the fabled hill

For me I'll take the raked
sand and boulders
of meditation

Dusk will soon start
stacking its boxes
of oncoming darkness

reminding me once more
that light is simply
the back-side of shadow

Fishing on Sylvan Lake

Lazy cane poles
    angle skyward
        willing to wait hours
for a single unsuspecting fish
    to take its bait

A mucky smell
    of dead fish
        roused by the warm sun
permeates partly-shaded water
    between willow branches

weeping trees that dance
    upside down
        in green water
as a sunfish splashes the surface
    to brandish its rainbow scales

A baby frog
    learns to jump
        from a lily pad
as bullfrogs full of brave adventure
    croak from the marshy shore

Dragon-flies hover
    over the white spires
        of tiny red-ball bobbers
little churches floating aloof
    responding to each jerk of the pole

sending out concentric ripples
    of communication
        to the rest of the world
that fishing here on Sylvan Lake
    is more than just catching a fish

Love Poem

He has spent the night in his studio
amid soaking brushes   tubes of glue

tearing odd-shaped scraps of paper
from old magazines and photographs

arranging and pasting them to a canvas
on which was inscribed his latest poem

a poem about love—remembering it   not
having it   wanting it   and wanting it bad

connecting power lines   high tension
wires ripped from their anchor towers

arcing beneath the deep cool of a cobalt sky
to the boxcars of freight trains   emerging

from mountain tunnels beneath neon signs
that read   *Café Blue   Electric Red*   pasting

them between the silhouettes of jazz bands
immersed in floating half-notes and smoky blues

As morning unfolds   he sits back   exhausted
amazed at how well the theme fits his poem

yet there are no icons of love   no hearts
no roses or boxes of chocolates   As he looks

at the electricity   the power of the locomotive
the tunnel   the freight cars   the smoky blues

jazz silhouettes   the flash of neon   blue and red
he murmurs   *I have come close to making love*

Always My Sea Nymph

My thoughts of you   and the moon
        in weightless orbits
                are heavy tonight
I can almost taste
        the low-tide smells
                of seaweed and loss

The self is nothing
        but an awareness
                of not belonging to anyone
 like shifting shadows
        ebbing tide-waves
                or scuttling sea creatures

take the lowly
        ashen sea apple who's
                never imagined a moon
yet gets all gussied up
        just to dine on plankton and get on
                with its job of self-reproduction

One must have a good understanding
        of love   to know whether
                or not it's being withheld
If you were here tonight I'd suggest
        we discard our clothes
                and walk barefoot in the sand

Night-games on Sylvan Lake

Water turns black
as night descends
over shattered boathouses
lining the once-wealthy
South Shore of Sylvan Lake
Rippled and ghost-like
they dance in the mirrored
silhouette of tree line
Tiny tongues of water
lap at empty rowboats
creaking out legends
in a lost language
to their moorings
The moon begins to play
games with a couple
of frisky clouds
while the sky fills with stars
and waits for someone
to connect-the-dots
of the dippers
We decide to join
the night-games
strip and let clothes fall
Hands enfolded we walk
the splintery surface
of the pier to its far end
Still holding hands
we make our big splash
into the intertwined arms
of a reflected universe

Sounds of the Night
—after Confusion of the Senses
by Kenneth Rexroth

Music of moonlight and stars
light the Night Jasmine
the air still and listening

The glow of our faces attract
We are opposite poles of a magnet
caught in a song of senses

that sees more than we can imagine
Your hair frames the features of a face
that blends with Monet's garden

Our lips close in on each other
Two lily pads whose stems
are tangled beneath the water-line

Our tongues willingly comingle
A night bird singing his moon-song
seems to know more than you or I

Your eyes are flames of celestial light
orbs of fire innocent as a fawn's
Your slender shoulders ripple

soft as breezes over the pond
arousing a scent of water lily
Naked together   we are alive

As Seen Through Smoked Glass

So much love is made
        then thrown back
like fish not big enough to keep
maybe a kiss or two short
        on the measuring stick

I can be easily bribed
        into believing beauty is truth
then the sky floods over
with a sweeping frustration
        of locusts

Time tightens most days
        like over-inflated toy balloons
contracts for brief periods of pleasure
and expands almost ruthlessly
        for pain and sorrow

A student sips Latte Macchiato
        with whipped cream
from a straw   hoping
it will help her tolerate
        organic chemistry

but whether or not her current
        love will last is a moot point
for the grooves of someone else's desire
have already been imprinted
        on her soul

By day our world seems limited
        the way the horizon
frames both land and sky
but night opens wide like a mouth
        wanting to show its tonsils

Both war and peace take breaks
          just long enough
to change the scenery and life itself
is nothing more than the mystery
          going on beneath

Day by Day

Evenings the sun
does its splash-less
belly flop
into a graying ocean
no steam or sizzle
of fire entering water

and such is life
a camel caravan
of optical illusions
hoping the next oasis
is not a mirage

nights following days
the turning on
and turning off of lights
praying we've raised
the bar a little
so we can sleep in peace

yet if we *are* growing
nothing tomorrow
will be any easier

This Old House

The end will never come
and then it's gone
like last April's mourning
sighing through louvered windows

We learn the art of lingering
spend hours with favorite fragrances
for time   like the wind
brings both and takes away

Like fine ashes we've heard stories
of those carried from us
so far away from home
if we can call this place home

It's hard to hide grief in a sugar bowl
so maybe we should
hope our handkerchiefs
soak up a world of sadness

And yet the moon manages
to keep on shining without much
of a reflective surface   she must know
more than she's willing to admit

It takes many grains
through the hourglass to heal a wound
but a tiny spark may
sometimes ignite a temperate love affair

We are thirsty souls   bread
leavened out of dust
heading like water
toward the comfort of sea level

Even at this very moment
while searching my sleeping son's face
for a trace of his grandfather   I wonder
if this old house will one day miss me

A Night-bird's Melody

The spotlight of desire shifts
like a searchlight looking for clues
to the breaking and entering
of my heart's chambers

as another chance at love ricochets
off my cold bottle of Corona
like a sidelong glance
from an adjacent barstool

She opened up at first like a book
I'd started   then lost my place
or maybe more like an old movie
I'd seen with one of my exes

Whoever framed my worldview
spinning so fast I can't justify the space
I occupy   should have known
I'd be better off nursing daydreams

I'll never divulge my whole story
even though I could recite it
from the early unplanned landscapes
to the trimmed hedges of today

We're loners when we arrive here
and loners when we leave
with a few acquaintances in between
that help define us

And since it's all win or lose
there are days when purpose leaves us
cold and flat   knowing silence
will get the biggest piece of the pie

So focus on the seeds of winter
now sprouting and beginning their slow
growth into longer lusher days
and stick with me   Baby

the hinged wings of my heart
will continue to flap about your flame
and like a night-bird's melody
mix with the far-flung stars

Brief Display of Fireworks

Brilliant streaks
of cyan and magenta

Burgeoning flowerets
of amber and purple

Anything to flood the night sky
with birthday candles

Then ash-rains commence
as the party burns out

Flakes of light ash continue
a determined descent

Transforming lingerers' faces
into petals of pallor-gray

Subtle reminders
of life's brief glow

Confessions of a Reformed Lover

I've spent years
leaping back and forth
over that wide wall between
Heaven and Hell
so before I break
the stained glass ceiling
and stand in repentance
face to face in front of God
I want to be sure I'm through
with my long nights
of dancing and getting drunk

Each drop of rain
bathes in its own puddle
leaving works of art
on the garden floor
I've learned that love
must be netted quickly
after being reeled in
or it will disappear faster than
the excitement of a rainbow trout
leaping into unfriendly air
above a mountain stream

When I set my mainsail loose
in uncharted skies
I hadn't realized how quickly
your scent of honey
would draw me back to the hive
where each evening after opening
our bedroom window
to the ocean's breeze
we slip in between satin sheets
and like the million stars above us
wait for our time to shine

Fear of Diving

I've never gone deep sea diving
but a recurring dream keeps telling me
I'd find untold sunken treasures
pirate chests spilling out gold doubloons
silver cutlery from captains' cabins
jewels and old watches from the trunks
of wealthy oil barons and their ladies
but my deep-seated fear of heavy helmets
and face masks as well as submergence
in deep water and total dependence
on a flimsy oxygen line that with one bite
by a man-eating shark could be severed
as the crew above looks on helplessly
at the ascending stream of air bubbles
has kept me from such adventuring
even though I know that Adrienne Rich
went diving in search of women's equality
and Stephen Dunn did it for love letters
And although Elizabeth Bishop may not
have gone diving herself   she believed
in total immersion for she was a Baptist
and she compares the briny taste of sea
water with knowledge   *dark   salt*
clear   moving   utterly free   which
might strike one as being somewhat odd
until she adds the part about how *knowledge*
is historical   hence *flowing and flown*
So maybe I should muster the courage
of a pirate or sea captain   don my mask
and conquer the great barrier reef of fear

Midnight Spelunking

Memory has a way of eroding
        like the aroma of an empty
scotch glass left on a nightstand

though I can still picture you
        in the bar staring at me
looking much like a question mark

then later confiding that fear
        is more easily concealed than
the desire to be loved

and our skin   it must be tough
        for it separates us from a weary
world   as well as from each other

We begin to explore the hollows
        of our hearts and the beats build
faster   then increasingly louder

Our bones begin to slink between
        the sheets with us still wrapped
ever so gently around them

and a day that began as a torn-open
        envelope is looking to end
in a quantum flicker of candlelight

Ode to Poets

Their survival depends on silver
    sprinkling cans
        as they cross-pollinate
from a parallel universe
    like bowed-down tulips
unsure of their own beauty

They know love stories
    make better kindling
        but fires soon flicker out
so they learn early on
    to fan the flames
with metaphor

Their angels are part
    messenger and part
        beast of burden
dwelling on how true spirit
    flies when stripped
of flesh and bones

Once through the worm hole
    they inhabit a single jewel
        in the bling of constellations
where the principle beauty
    of butterflies
lies in their un-punctuated wings

A Poet's Creed

I hereby vow
    to create new worlds

separate light
    from darkness

or maybe darkness
    from light

build new heavens
    and new earths

populate them
    with angels and imps

the sky I create
    will be my firmament

and I will honor
    the craft of poetry

and bless those poems
    who carry out my will

Pantoum of Bedside Notes

I cannot remember things once read or dreamed
which explains the note pad I keep close to my bed
for morning arrives and things aren't what they seemed
as fragments of images swim through my head

which explains the note pad I keep close to my bed
Fat Cats and Gun Molls and sirens that screamed
as fragments of images swim through my head
handcuffs and jailbirds with no one redeemed

Fat Cats and Gun Molls and sirens that screamed
I try to make sense of these cheap books I've read
handcuffs and jailbirds with no one redeemed
or did they sneak out of my nightmares instead

I try to make sense of these cheap books I've read
I've used magic to turn them to poems that gleamed
or did they sneak out of my nightmares instead
pink elephants   henchmen   confetti that streamed

I've used magic to turn them to poems that gleamed
mixing back-alley blues with the highly-unbred
pink elephants   henchmen   confetti that streamed
I ache like I've been to the Land of the Dead

Mixing back-alley blues with the highly-unbred
for morning arrives and things aren't what they seemed
I ache like I've been to the Land of the Dead
I cannot remember things once read or dreamed

Remembering Tears

There's bee salt and sea salt and NaCl
though taste varies slightly we know it so well

There's salt in our system it's been there for years
It's mostly contained but it leaks out in tears

I've tasted a few and they're filled with emotion
aroused by our origin deep in the ocean

This of course is what scientists tell us
My minister says they're a bit over-zealous

When tears due to happiness cloud up the eyes
they have a sweet taste   that to me's no surprise

For I once knew a girl with a cinnamon flavor
who shed tears of joy which I still fondly savor

So I remind young folks as they grow in years
to number their blessing   remember their tears

The Red Folding Chair

I like being the only red
among the other drab grays
I stand out   I shine
as sunrays filter through
the Venetian blind of pine needles
just beyond our library window

Poets gather here once a week
which brings in a lot of excitement
but my hopes are dashed
as the blond poet in her tight skirt
pink sweater and pearls   always
chooses the chair *next* to me

Maybe she thinks I clash with her colors
I always get the heavy-set bald guy
who thinks he's spinning gold from straw
but couldn't write a good poem if he had to
Not that I'm a critic   but I've been
unfolded   set up   folded back again

then stacked here in this corner for years
In the meantime I've learned a lot
about image   metaphor   and simile
Once in a while they'll discuss a poem
or two written by some famous poet
I like the one about the red wheelbarrow

I keep wishing that one of these poets
might come up with something like
So much depends on a red
folding chair   soaked in cold sweat
holding up the heavy-set poet
next to the pink sweater

The Tarvy

Who wouldn't love
you   America
and not just your flag
your statue   your
great stone faces   nor
your purple mountains
and fruited plains
I'm talking
about the narrow
hollyhock-lined path
from the kitchen porch
with its rusted screen door
always slamming
down past the three-holer
outhouse   then on out
through the remnants
of the family garden
dying potato vines
onions gone to seed
a few zinnias and marigolds
in the first row
always reserved for
the best mother
in the world
through the weeds
of the back alley and out
onto the Old Canal Road
the only paved one
in our part of town
we called it The Tarvy
it was our way out

To My Leading Lady

Since you exited stage left   I understand
        why critics tend to amplify
                the void of a few empty seats

Your reassuring lips once spoke of passion
        and a single breath in the ear
                could cause costumes to tumble

Now consumed by my own petty scripts
        I pursue dwindling accolades
                to unmet dreams

I practice life behind a closed curtain
        as I hide among its pleats
                from fading footlights

Summer seasons seem shorter
        as July sweeps up her days
                like last night's ticket stubs

Roles drag about like waifs in tattered
        costumes   over-directed and filled
                with miscue after miscue

Even the sunset's scarred face is painted over
        in pink makeup   trying to cover up
                blushes from hisses and boos

Tomorrow I'll give another unrehearsed
        performance and hopefully
                nurse one more standing ovation

Apple Trees of Boyhood Pantoum

It was scary to climb in those dazzling spring trees
still flowers of the memory come back to bloom
he could hear the loud buzzings of thousands of bees
if they'd all stung at once it would surely mean doom

still flowers of the memory come back to bloom
though bark could be rough on a little boy's knees
if they'd all stung at once it would surely mean doom
yet nothing compared to that sweet-apple breeze

though bark could be rough on a little boy's knees
one swing from a limb took away all the gloom
yet nothing compared to that sweet-apple breeze
he was watchful but never thought twice of the tomb

one swing from a limb took away all the gloom
braved it like pirates who ruled the high seas
he was watchful but never thought twice of the tomb
a sure guarantee that his friends wouldn't tease

braved it like pirates who ruled the high seas
his crow's nest on high gave him plenty of room
a sure guarantee that his friend wouldn't tease
till that day he fell out and landed ker-BOOM

his crow's nest on high gave him plenty of room
he could hear the loud buzzings of thousands of bees
till that day he fell out and landed ker-BOOM
It was scary to climb in those dazzling spring trees

Harbinger of Spring

Each year by February
even the children began to tire
of stubborn Indiana winters
that wouldn't surrender

Once-white crystalline snow
turned gray with soot
slushy by day   re-freezing
into clinkers overnight

My mother kept a sharp eye peeled
for the first robin
claimed it was a sure sign
spring was on its way

She told the myth
of how the robin singed his breast
when stealing fire from the sun
to bring it back to earth

The year the first robin and its mate
decided to build their nest
outside our kitchen window
helped her forget winter woes

The bright-hued male
brought sticks and bits of string
while the female poked
and tucked at the loose ends

They worked for days
weaving a three-dimensional
canvas with an artistic wash
of browns and grays

The perfect background
for their crop of heavenly-blue eggs
extending a season
of enhanced joy to a mother's life

Annual Spring Dance

Perfumed in pink chiffon
the apple trees of spring
dress for the onslaught
of their cocksure bow-tied bees
who come courting in tuxes
doing their fertile dances
of cross-pollination
in search of sweet nectar
to feed their hungry hives

In the wake of mating season
floral sacs that once flaunted
petals   sepals and stamens
lie alone and naked with nothing
to do but morph into fleshy fruits
which in their hours of ripeness
are jewels of an orchard destined
to remain barren until its trees
doll up again next spring

Magic of the Night

Shot like fire-tipped arrows
    by some mythical archer

through a millennium
    of space-time sprinkled

with billions of possible other-worlds
    brings up many

questions about our unique
    life on Earth

and fosters science fiction
    while creating a few

fissures in parochial religious
    constructs and beliefs

of God   so just relax into
    the romantic nature of

starlight and enjoy its universal
    magical light-show

The Royal Aspens

Under the bluest of blue November skies
        autumn is about to jump off the cliff again
leaving behind her swarms of fallen leaves

once a budding then full-open green going
        yellow and crimson in the night by frost
still seen lurking in the lush shrubbery of day

The aspen tree by our front gate was always
        the first one to release its leaves because
of their impatient quaking all summer long

The neighborhood children knew the myths
        told of aspens doomed by the gods to quiver
as a result of white lies or minor disobedience

But I remember my grandfather telling me over
        and over that the aspen leaves had royal blood
in their veins and so they waved like queens

And when he said it was time to clean them up
        we grabbed rakes and began building stacks
for frolicking in   before lighting our bonfires

When I look back at the life cycles of the leaves
        veins growing prominent and losing flexibility
prior to changing costumes for their curtain calls

then even more brittle before turning to ash
        I notice the quivering of my own veined hands
think of our aspen and wave to her like royalty

Unless Venus Intervenes

The space between us
is like an opening of lips
longing for closure

As hungry as two distant
stars in a binary system stuck
in their wobbly orbit

An empty reach where fear hangs
in a bundle of dark matter
dripping slowly

like petals being pulled
from a flower
by some uncertain lover

wanting love to speak back
in her simple vocabulary
of meteors and comets

turn tables on God's telescope
face the bright white
like a deer in the headlights

for too much distance could
damage both of us
unless Venus

telegraphs an urgent message
to Earth's moon regarding
her notion of closeness

and to Earth a notion
of stepping back from its
bungled romantic scripting

quit reminding us we are nothing
but drawn out tails hiding
in the wakes of lustful comets

burning out as we enter
this unfriendly atmosphere
of unbridled infidelity

Early Morning Meditation

From our bed at dawn
the rhythm slows to a robin's
early morning oratorio
reminding us we inhabit a planet
without umbilical cords
knowing time will accomplish
his tasks without our help

Within the medium of air
we breathe   complete silence
at best a myth   and serenity
merely a line-item
on our way to enlightenment
where we begin to view life
as the stillness of a wall painting

Poetry can be perceived
in a wedged formation of pelicans
written using an alphabet
inscribed in the clouds
and a minor change
in one of our primary colors
will alter the world's complexion

We know the edge
of contentment ebbs and flows
like an ocean's tide
so why not etch our initials
on the walls of each others' hearts
and let them mirror love's
unlimited levitation

Fresh Breath of Vibrations

There are those who say
the human race runs on dice
and mathematics
but I think it's more like
a fresh breath of vibrations

Our life story didn't begin
on a torn piece of napkin
nor one of those
iridescent-soap-bubble promises
that always pop too soon

The baggage we thought
we'd need to get where we wanted
to go   got heavier
and heavier as we headed toward
that place we've yet to find

and just as we began to think
there was nothing more beautiful
than nearness in the dark
the mote-filled fingers of dawn
filtered through our blinds

but then   the music began
to fill the air with a freshness
and our willingness blended
into a harmony of colors
from ultra-violet to infra-red

assuring us that the vaulted sky
still carries its dippers   bears
and huntsman   almost like
fingerprints on a treasured
family photo album

Hope

A harmonic chord
of sunlight
filters through the trees
like a dream
meant to be recycled
so the earth can show
its brighter side again
as storm clouds
un-paste themselves
from a billboard sky
and the settled lake
begins to shimmer
like wrinkled tinfoil

Humanity . . .

that temporal ballast
which imprisons
collective spirit   splits it

segregates and isolates
traps it behind worldly bars
forces each fragment

to wander aimlessly
as unwilling companion
to its assigned human host

is   in the end   the ultimate loser
as   one by one   each fragment
cries out   stretches   snaps

its earthly bonds and reunites
in cosmic ecstasy with the whole
depositing its worn out vehicles

in the refuse pile of time   without
even a single sigh from the lower
forms of life here on Earth

I am

Two little words
that glorify the state
of being alive

Sunflowers offer them
in their wide smiles
of yellow petals

Honeybees buzz them
as they dart above
the dahlias

Wolves howl them out
as they bay
at a ghostly moon

You and I express them
by deep-diving
into a lingering kiss

The day *I am* dismantles
is a day nobody knows
nor will remember

In Need of a Pied Piper

We are a planet of discarded wings
adrift on a sea of molten rock
following the second hand as it dips
into each new moment

Our cells have sense enough
to do their exquisite jobs on their own
that is   until death sneaks in
like a sudden undeserved hailstorm

Midnights wrap around us
like questioning quilts hammering out
dreams and nightmares   nothing more
than gathered stories from our past

I like to hang out on those remembered
porches of childhood
where neighborhood kids lost their shoes
and clamored the summers away

It is said that smooth stones make the best
mementos if we value endurance
but I'd rather have letters from a broken
alphabet filling my jewelry box

I'm aware of the many blessings astir
in my bloodline and yet I'm nothing more
than the extended honeymoon
of some ancient sperm-egg marriage

How to End a Poem

Holding a cup of frozen
yogurt in one hand
and a plastic spoon in the other
I shovel away
as though I'm knee-deep
in the blizzard of '79

Each bite seems to taste better
than the previous one
so as I come to the end
and gulp down
that last spoonful
I tilt the cup to scrape its sides
and scrounge
for what isn't even there

So when I write my next poem
I need to remember
to hand the spoon over
just before that last bite
so my reader can have a taste
of what I am trying to say

From a Bridge at Night
Overlooking the Elkhart River

I know these dark waters
        waded them bank to bank
                in my father's extra hip boots
and they're way too shallow
        to hold the inexhaustible and blazing
                stars that go down so deep
deeper than the catfish and carp
        those bottom feeders who skim
                the mud in search of nourishment

One of the more blissful fish
        perhaps a bass or bluegill leaps
                upward with high-jumper skill
as the reflected stars shuffle outward
        showing a little nervousness
                before finally settling
into the vast cosmic stillness of night
        to gaze back at our universe
                and help me fish for my father

Aphrodite

Goddess of love   beauty and pleasure
        protector of sea-faring men
You rose from the froth of the sea
        floated ashore in your oyster shell
bringing love into an untidy world
        irresistible icon to both men and gods
Not that I ever wanted to be a sailor
        but when you drift about my room
with a soft and unsinkable serenade
        just to breathe new life
into my tattered and patched old sails
        I taste the long-lost salt on my lips
reel to the crash of each brash new wave
        against my steadfast pillow
adjust my sea-legs to life's new rhythms
        and ask you to dance

Lover with Hat

An empty hat somebody left on the chair
          next to mine in Starbucks
                    kept me company all afternoon

Said she'd spent her morning dilly-dallying
          among meadow flowers that swayed
                    in the wind like yellow balloons

An invisible curtain of rain
          with its unmistakably bold aroma
                    of enhanced oxygen unfolded

It was as though a confetti
          of migrating monarch butterflies
                    had been loosed from the far hills

And the dandelions long past bloom were
          wispy spheres of unlaunched parachutes
                    ghosts holding communion

She told me that dreams needed legs
          so they can skip and run
                    but then they sometimes escape us

I'm dreaming your owner will return
          happy to find you still waiting
                    and join us for a Caramel Macchiato

Then when a more-than-half-dark moon
          appears above the horizon
                    the three of us will stroll in the park

We'll pose by the fountain where darkness lurks
          and you   slung back will inspire
                    a long embrace and drawn-out kiss

Long enough to be turned to bronze ourselves
        on display for the people who will name us
                perhaps *Lovers with Hat*

Then from out of nowhere a wrinkled crone appears
        My hat   my hat   My dream takes legs
                streaks away   without looking back

Bus Ride

In my dream I'm riding on a Greyhound bus
The year is 1956 somewhere in Mississippi
and this I know for a fact because the black lady
sitting next to me is going over her wallet calendar
from the Biloxi Walgreen Pharmacy

We share a seat near the center
of the crowded bus   right at the dividing line
between blacks and whites   We talk
I don't remember who spoke first
but as we pass a car dealership featuring

those fancy new two-tone Ford Fairlanes
I point one out   robin's egg blue and cream
as I recall   with lots of chrome stripping
I tell her I can't wait to graduate from Ol' Miss
so I can afford one of these luxury cars

She smiles and says she can't wait to experience
the thrill of sitting in the front section of the bus
I wake up in California some forty years later
and realize her wish has come true   but me
I'm still ripping around in an old VW Golf

Only a Dream*

Mrs. Hemmingway
in her signature straw hat
scarf   and horned-rim-glasses
stands and stares at me like a doll
made from a wooden spoon
I tell her *I am a town*
just one step ahead of my wild blue
and sometimes checkered past
on *the dreaming road* to future
I let poetry fill each room
of my existence *between here and gone*
The pond I swim in is an adjective
its shoreline crowded with verbs
Come on come on and play   I say
as I splash my spray against
virgin shores   we all need a few chains
the challenge to escape them
You cast a shadow as well as anyone
My attic is crammed with the stuff
of creation   2 X 4s   planks
and sexy tongue-and-grooves
I fan away any fog that nags
hoping   the air I breathe
the food I eat   will remember me
My daily choreographies of position
power   affection and desire
are like the friendly smoke   curling
up from autumn bonfires
When my resolutions fizzle
like wet fireworks   and my *ideas*
are like stars we see   but are already
dead   *when time stands still*
like a field of corn   *on and on it goes*
tassels pressed against the sky

absolutely nothing changing
I lay down my defenses   and snuggle
into the cradle of Mother Earth
saying   *Goodnight   America*

***Note: Italicized phrases are titles of the ten songs
on the 2014 album   *Songs From The Movie*
by Mary Chapin Carpenter**

Smoldering Torches

Summers after sundown
we sat in the bent meadow grass
slapping mosquitos

pretending the thousands of blinking
fireflies were neural-firings from a great
spirit   spreading long-held secrets

and if we stared long and hard
we'd come to know everything
there was to know

Some evenings we gathered cattails
from the swamp out beyond Emerson's
muck farm to soak in kerosene

and with touch of match elevate them
to torches   advancing us to cavemen
mentality as we paraded with fire

down Milnor's lane and through wheat fields
beyond   panting as we ascended Becker's
Hill to where we fell among clover

beneath a silent moon that could neither see
nor hear us   ditched our smoldering flares
and began kindling fires from within

Tunnel of Love

It wasn't just the name of the ride
nor the long-haired eerie carnival barker
white-faced and tuxedoed that hooked us
in each year along that seedy second-tier
midway of the Noble County Fair next
to the Sword Swallower and Bearded Lady
It was the mandatory kissing that went on
If a guy didn't emerge with a little
lipstick smeared on his face or neck
he was jeered by boys in sophomore class
Kissing began as soon as our boats
slipped into the slow-moving stream
of stagnant   polluted water
starting with simple hand and forehead
kisses   then Eskimo   French and
butterfly kisses   single-lip   ear-lobe
and lingering kisses   nibble   lizard
seductive kisses   out of breath   yet
more out of breath kisses   kisses until
feet on ground   *terra firma*   hardly
in love but feeling as though spoken to
by joyful voices from another world

Bridge to Nowhere

We once stood
      on the bridge
that spanned the slough

below us
      the moon's reflected
strip of tarnish

added a bit of glamour
      to the bilge and backwash
of high tide

and we savored
      the sea salt settling in
between our lips

Then dredgers came
      and turned the slough
into a lagoon

the once eucalyptus-lined
      road was widened
and guard rails added

and the bridge
      shut to thru traffic
became a viewpoint

then you too were taken
      leaving me on a bridge
to nowhere

Double Fault

I'm hoping you'll bounce back some day
        like some lost tennis ball
jump into my court   resume the play
I'm hoping you'll bounce back some day
bring sunlit skies   discount the gray
        our game was great before the fall
I'm hoping you'll bounce back some day
        like some lost tennis ball

I hear your whispers   feel their touch
        though we are miles apart
nights drag through   not leaving much
I hear your whispers   feel their touch
lost love is like a splintered crutch
        or maybe like an armored heart
I hear your whispers   feel their touch
        though we are miles apart

We'll fly to Wimbledon to wed
        drink wine from a silver cup
forgive each other for things we've said
We'll fly to Wimbledon to wed
In an English manor we'll take to bed
        till tea and crumpets wake us up
We'll fly to Wimbledon to wed
        drink wine from a silver cup

Love Needs a Little Needling

Those instants I want to hold onto so dearly
      are always the ones that slip through my fingers
The many things my mother uttered
      that were never meant to hurt me
or holding hands with you across that bare Formica table
      of our first unfurnished apartment

Early morning light has cast its net again
      over this sleepy neighborhood's steep roofs
sending sun rays bouncing off the tiles
      like shattered shards of ice during hailstorms
There's a sting in the air and a taste of honey
      but the buzz is gone from the hive

Love must be like water   taking on the shape
      of whatever surrounds it
and if you tried holding it in your hand   it too
      would slip right through your fingers
Long-lasting love kits include patching-up needles
      but ours seemed to have lost its thread

We mustn't forget that we too are mostly water
      searching for comfortable containers
So the point of this letter is to ask for your forgiveness
      and to invite you back into the hive
As containers of love for each other   I promise
      to keep our needle well-threaded

Amber Silence

We're here on a blanket
        watching white puffy clouds
wither   then change shape
        as they accumulate

Just offshore   breakers stretch
        and fall to their knees
like flocks of seagulls
        surfing gusty wind currents

Much of this world
        is hard to understand at times
but lying here with you
        seems to offset all worries

Our life together
        has attained an oceanic richness
that most ships
        will never learn to navigate

As the water darkens
        beneath a more calming sky
a long-necked bird
        wades into twilight

to a depth
        you and I know well
for we have ventured there
        together

Later we'll be holding hands
        in candlelight
letting the rest of the world
        slide by in amber silence

Butterfly Kisses

When we first met   your gauzy
glances turned my sinewy membranes
to ashes and I felt as though I'd
perhaps invented sculpted glass
It's the story of a simple man expecting
the woman of his dreams to embrace him
and you did just that   We threw coins
 into places where pigeons were splashing
Sometimes you listened carefully to me
like a good silk dress in church
and other times you were as elusive
as one of the ghosts of Rome   When I
told you I'd never been served champagne
in a glass slipper   and you said you owned
a pair   my body burst into flames
like a wheat field in Tuscany   afire
with blood-red poppies   It's hard to know
if we're floating along with the Tiber
or standing on the bank watching it go by
But didn't someone say that wisdom
is mostly knowing what to overlook
So many blank pages await us in this world
we must remind ourselves over and over
to try to forget those dog-eared ones
Thoughts like these seem to line up
and then complain about the extended wait
I sometimes feel like a printed page longing
to be cursive   Just think   a caterpillar kiss
could never make it at a time like this
that's why butterflies are so lucky   Here
bring your face in   just a little bit closer
That's it   Perfect   Now blink

Poppies

—When you take a flower
in your hand and really look at it,
it's your world for the moment
Georgia O'Keeffe

Somewhere
in Antelope Valley
not too far
off State Road 138
in California
we came upon
a panacea of poppies
heavily populated
with people
and since we could not
shoot a panorama
we opted for
a Georgia O'Keeffe
portrait of nature
a close-up into lovers' eyes
where sharp lines
almost disappear
deep starburst centers
staring back
transfixing us
in a space
of fluttering wings
tangerine and gold
begging us
in this brief encounter
for butterfly kisses

I am Apple

fleshy and tempting
born from delicate beauty
of a single blossom abuzz
with frenzied bees
in search of heavenly nectar
who   in their scurrying
tracked pollen over parts
of my mother-flower
no longer hidden by
a pink-petalled skirt
to pollinate her
in scaled-down flurry
of sexual consummation
thus bearing me
a tiny fruitlet
which would develop through
the green adolescence
of late spring into rosy
middle-aged summer
and on into ripening autumn
and whether plucked and eaten
or left to fall and ferment
I've played my part
in the grand mystery of life
and stored its eternal secrets
deep within my core

Autumn Comes to Brock's Woods

The yellow leaves
of poplars
so still and silent
in the first rays
of morning
take up a seemingly
unimportant rustling
as cool autumn air
from across the meadow
reaches the only place
they've known
since birth

A few let go
of the mother trees
who have spent their
entire spring and summer
supplying sustenance
to their growing
broods
of playful babies
attendant
in the growth of each
from bud to quaking
leaf

And when the rain arrives
in final encouragement
of the hangers-on
to join their comrades' fate
among the growing patches
of carpet now covering
most of the forest floor
one does begin to wonder

if they had been hoping
for this breeze
and maybe even praying
for this rain

Sonnet for Lake Erie

They warned us storms rose up like ghosts at night
yet still we ventured far from Erie's shore
so sure we were that love would scare off fright
and love is what we both were longing for

Too soon the clouds rolled in and weather changed
as whitecaps grew and splashed their wrath in pools
the contents of our boat were disarranged
we lost both oars and felt like hapless fools

but when we saw our boat had sprung a leak
she said there's nothing left to do but pray
then through the clouds the sun began to peek
the answer to our prayers had saved the day

and this we learned about the power of love
It calms the waves yet comes from up above

Early Adolescence

It all begins suddenly like a sunflower
awakening from the morning dew
when a dawning creeps over
a teenage girl's horizon by surprise
emanating a scent of ripening often found
in the upper-most branches of cherry trees
causing the boys   itchy in their jeans
to rise from their slouched positions
and march to the silent drumbeats
swelling within their own bodies
and like peacocks spreading tail feathers
during mating season   they are certain
they'll find their life-long lovers
through scent and sound alone
Both sexes are prone to overspend
from the un-funded banks of their minds
Blurred words fall from journal pages
like frazzled fluff as they try to weave them
back into the soft fabric of a security blanket
Lightning cuts through the very air
they breathe like a whetted razor-sharp wind
They straddle the back of an untamed horse
that somehow has appeared out of nowhere
and ride roughshod through rocky ravines
until they are bucked off into sagebrush
bruised and battered but back on the trail

Enjoy the Journey...

for despite the
occasional
tears
the dance will
swing
toward laughter

just as music
moves
toward silence
where it
hangs
momentarily

bodiless and
simpler
than the inhaled
space
between
conversations

more
peaceful
than the empty
sanctuary
after worshipers
have filed out

as we edge
toward death
like hillsides trying
to hold onto
that last bit of
sunlight

we enter a new
phase of our journey
so offer a smile
and bow to the oarsman
in charge
of the crossing

Femme Fatale

Last night loneliness crept
    into my king-size bed
        like a familiar stranger
using her old dishonest lines to reconnect

She wore the wistful face
    of a restless moon
        then held out an offer
to unload my luggage-bound soul

Drawstrings of another day
    had just been pulled tight
        A crumpled cigarette package
on the floor by my bed seemed to annoy her

Beware of love   she advised
    for it can snatch a fragile heart
        and wring it dry   leave it
like the twisted bedsheet you've become

True love can be as pure and serene
    as a deep mountain lake
        but the first fires of an affair
require a ridiculous amount of kindling

When love finally flakes off
    like bark of Eucalyptus
        dark puddles within your eyes
take in whatever is given them

Once asleep   I dream you've come back
    and our love-making has re-grooved
        like an overly-repeated prayer
ending in Hallelujah rather than Amen

Now tomorrow   burned out
   and with a taint of ash
      still lingering on my tongue
you pop up in every pretty face I pass

Moonlight

There are times
      when the windows
to my recent past
      get fogged over
or boarded up

and the heart
      of the moon
loses its pulse
      yet even with
what's left of her

borrowed light
      she can lead me
like a will-o'-the-wisp
      down the darkest
of alleys

My Longest Day
—*upon the burial of*
my sister Sally (1938 – 2015)

It began on a hill
before the wind came
with its somber message
of unburdening another
earth-bound treasure
by a single angel
whose job it was
to take my sister
leaving me with grief
and this slow drive
through narrow streets
of the dead
where over-shadowing
red cedar pines point
to a broken sky
and my mind goes back
to that summer day we lay
on our backs exhausted
in a plowed field
just east of Kneipp Springs
Nunnery
after a blistering day
of planting seedling pines
for a Christmas tree farm
and the flute-strains flowing
from a Nun on the far hill
Now the Day is Over

My Only Escape

I want to run
from those persistent feelings
          emerging
from loneliness of nights
which I can never seem to shake
          this world of self
where each square mile
is packed with strangers
          and collapse of meaning

Escape these hinterlands
of nameless fears
          where future's unknowns
outnumber equations of past
and present
          My time peering
through self-constructed
prison bars
          has reshaped me

into an echo of the man I was
yet some feelings still dangle
          like flimsy motel coat hangers
making me want to flee entirely
Instead I settle in
          beneath un-starred skies
and wait to dip
and dive into those swirly pools
          of your magnetic eyes

The Fountain Within

A front-page picture features a wrinkled
woman playing her concert grand piano

The article points out how her hands
develop memory as a result of practice

And though her brain has been ravaged
she still plays a skillful Beethoven Sonata

Effect of aging on the human condition
is a new point of focus for entrepreneurs

Yes   the quest for the *fountain of youth*
is still bright and shining in Silicon Valley

A hedge fund has set up a multi-million
dollar prize to 'hack the code of life'

One subsidiary of Google has a mission
to reverse-engineer the human lifespan code

Science is trying hard to shake the world
out of its ageing-is-unavoidable 'trance'

A company called Human Longevity plans
to map the genomes of supercentenarians

Aging needs to be attacked at its roots
rather than addressed one disease at a time

In the meantime I sit wringing my hands
not remembering what they once longed for

The Relay Race

The *me* of day tries hard
to make the room turn about him
dragging everyone else along
faster and faster until the universe
is spinning about the *me* of day

The *me* of night tries hard
to slow things down with the help
of a gin and tonic then after several
 the race resumes and soon
the *me* of night is spinning
about the bottle   hoping to land
a long-planned kiss on you

The *me* of day and the *me*
of night in our relay race toward
nothingness silently pass each other
and hand our baton back and forth
knowing we shall never become one

Where Love and Greed Collide

Alms for the Poor was the sign he held
because he was
crippled and couldn't work

Desperate   by the bank he sat
expecting a buck   not a
flippin' smirk

Grateful for pennies and dimes received
humiliation a small price to pay
in diminishing the school kids' lunches

just enough to get him by
Kind   it was   for kids to share
like pigeons they came at noon in bunches

Maybe move closer to the school
needless to say it made more sense
On the other hand   here he stays within

potential reach of a CEO
Queer how cash sways poor and
rich in different ways   charity   greed's sin

Sometimes after school is out
the bank closed for the day   he waits
until the sun sinks out of sight

ventures to the park where his small
world collides with society's and stamps his
X on a bench for the night

Yearning not   he counts his sheep
Z's are the alms that let him sleep

Writing Memoir

All night long
stars have been sprouting
        like fresh mint
in my long-neglected herb garden

which I know
will be bankrupt by summer's end
        leaving bouquets
so faint they'll be difficult to trace

It's the story
that defines the seasons of a lifetime
        the give and take
between blurred myth and reality

but for now
it percolates in early morning light
        and my in-basket
sits waiting for the windfall

I pay attention
to my ravenous appetite for flavor
        pry open
the back door of past as best I can

search deep
for how I wished things were
        so we'll have
no excuses not to dance again

but as my pen's
spotlight flickers in and out of focus
        I find some scenes
are badly blotched with graffiti

as if fate is wanting
to trim back my overblown ego
and cover up
any earthy metaphors for love

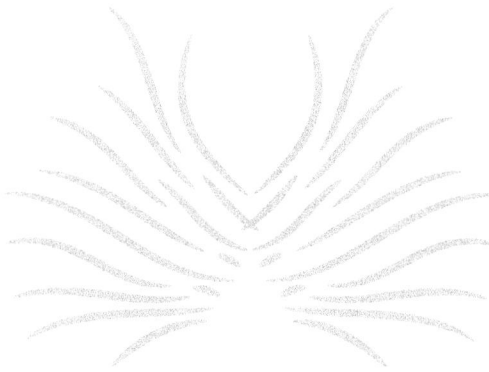

A Little Learning

after An Essay on Criticism
—Alexander Pope

Autumn loosens its grip again
        and another year lumbers by
                like a load of clover hay
The students are back in line
        the chalkboard filled
                erased then filled again
The ivy that hallows these halls
        hangs over the window
                like an untamed eyebrow
Over her half-rimmed glasses
        Miss Biggerstaff paces and lectures
                passing on what she knows

Imprints of your footsteps will trail
        behind you whether or not
                flowers adorn your path
Never alienate yourselves from nature
        the tide pools are waiting to become
                part of the incoming tide
If you can't be free as a bird
        be a mystery of interlocking twigs
                that is suddenly a nest
The most you can hope for is to become
        like a fist paused in mid-air
                always prepared to knock
For the world will gladly open its offerings
        of pre-measured magic shoes
                ready to fit able and willing feet

Hints From the Heavens

Each day another unedited
          page in our manuscript
                    is thoroughly read through
and swallowed whole
          before the tide of night
                    can rise to flood-stage

No doubt there is meaning in the stars
          so many light-years away
                    a meaning that creates
love-chatter among the night-birds
          and turns frog-croaking
                    into prayers of jubilation

When darkness hovers over the geography
          and daffodils are brought
                    to their knees by dew
remember how the arms of an oak tree
          if only for a brief moment
                    can cradle the moon

Absorbing and Being Absorbed

—Life is a long road on a short journey
James Lendall Basford

That long letter I wrote you last night in my dream
      was actually a poem I've wished
           all morning I could remember

It pretty much meandered like the complex paths
      we take on our brief journeys
           from birth to death

I admitted being infected by a love with no known cure
      but who in their right mind
           would want one

that I was a man of many moods trying to accept life
      as it hurries along merrily absorbing
           and being absorbed

while Death   that unpaid actor waits in the wings
      only barging onto the stage for final
           curtain call and applause

Awake now   I sit here wondering if lust will ever lose
      its luster as your picture on my desk keeps
           shouting   *Look at me*

Acquiring Faith the Hard Way

21 now she presses her tear-stained face to a window
her heart a snail on the sidewalk waiting to be crushed

She grew up in an orchard where the fruit ripened slowly
among a mix of people afraid to flaunt their true personas

She still recalls the first glimpse of her mama's green eyes
and the relentless sunshine of that untamed orange-red hair

The meadows of her life had become pastures of confusion
until that night Lover's Lane snatched her out of adolescence

Her eyes whispered sweet promises not meant to be honored
reminiscent of those hand-written love notes she'd never sent

Instead of trying to remodel her broken record of bad dreams
she became a harp that needed to be caressed with both hands

Love was reduced to a sculptor molding male egos into hers
by shifting their shapes like an expert in wet clay and plaster

She flirted through local taverns chiseling out a reputation
that no man in this county would cross her path unscathed

Clearly   lust had pitched its tent in a clearing of her mind
and told her   *Taste me and I'll dance on your lips forever*

She learned too late that only a jail-break out of her anatomy
would give her a faith deeper than any stain on her skirt

Any Town...

is a drinking town
filled
with unquenchable flame
unmet desire

beached whales
struggling
toward an inviting ocean
drag along holders-on
like you and me

and all the others
huddled here
hidden from sunlight
nosing through imagined
seaweed

deeper
and deeper still
as one glass empties
another one begins

John Barleycorn

Joe and I knew him
only too well
but so did Bud and Louise

He always sat
at the other end of the bar
What a loser

And no wonder,
he was the ugliest fellow
to ever come in this place

Bulbous red nose
roadmap eyes
kangaroo pouch of a stomach

The bartender warned us
Beware   he's a true plunderer
his insatiate wants are contagious

But what a weakling
we used to think   even Louise
could take him down

Years later in an AA meeting
with Joe   Bud and Louise
we agree   *John Barleycorn*
          that bastard

Global Warming

Some Eye   from God-knows-where
may one day zero in on us
and stare   where we once grew
from Eden's womb
and loved   and toiled   and fought
and yet what little care
we gave our planet went for naught
and wonder at the arid signatures
of oceans lakes and streams
epigraphs of nature left to mark a rocky
tomb   with temperatures outside
the range of life as primal beings know it
yet giant pyramid shapes
in scattered places   seem to show it
Perhaps a troubled expedition
with no power to reach its mother ship
set up shop in a deep-down maze
with pyramid power to bounce away
the cosmic rays   and tele-transport
lines for their supplies   This is not a place
for us to colonize   for there are many
planets with environs friendlier than these
and so the word to X us out was no surprise
and yet a tiny tear forms in the Eye
                from God-knows-where
                        that no one sees

Homeless Woman Rondeau

A homeless woman who combs her hair
a few teeth missing   she doesn't care
but it's rare that a mirror can ever be found
so she preens in cracked windows   so many abound
for the prince who'll come searching for his lady fair

She always seems happy   no time for despair
a full grocery cart and an orange-crate chair
the world throws away things for her to be found
a homeless woman who combs

So what can I do if I feel I should share
greet her with kindness and don't ever stare
but can't I do something to make her more sound
or must I accept she'll be hangin' around
running this way and that   both here and there
a homeless woman who combs

In Flight

When they finally decided to erase their reasons
from the bedroom walls and neutralize
the overlapping chemistry of their shadows
they noticed how the cellophane moon
stared down over silhouetted hills
in wonderment of silence and meaning
copulating in semi-darkness
They had hoped the angels wouldn't wince
or frown as they dreamed of crawling through
fire to be purified even though camouflaging
a myth for the Promised Land of no befores
or afters might simply create a new myth
and that's why they decided to dump it all
into the trash bin of misguided ideas
including those semi-precious commodities
of frail fantasies and brute obsessions
As they parted ways a wedge of honking
southbound geese split the cool November air
Neither of them bothered to look up

Kindhearted Soul

My father never talks about God
nor Jesus nor anything vaguely religious
but my mother tells me and my sister
as we walk the five or so blocks
to First Baptist Church each Sunday
Don't worry about your father
he's really a very kind-hearted soul
and she always says the same thing
whenever he breakes one of his promises
to take us to a street fair or the movies
only to end up in one of the local taverns
I don't think she's ever considered the fact
that I might be worrying more about me
I can't live up to my sister's standards
She always goes back to evening services
and attends Wednesday prayer meetings
Reverend Goodman says my life will change
if I would just follow in my sister's footsteps
and accept Jesus Christ as my personal savior
but I have other things to think about and do
I just want to be left alone even if it means
I will burn in Hell for my lies which I know
are just cover-ups for some of the greater sins
of adolescence with all of its unbuckling of belts
and loosening of blouses and so stubbornness
convinces me to put off   at least for now
becoming that sort of wishy-washy nice guy
my mother might call a kind-hearted soul

Lady Liberty

A frothy wake of water
stretches from the stern
of the U.S.S. General Walker
back toward New York Harbor
where you stand adrift in the shoals
of your honor   guarding against
slavery   oppression   tyranny
right foot raised ever so slightly
as though about to step down
from your pedestal and put a smile
on that stern-looking face of yours
perhaps throw down the torch
and toss your seven-spiked crown
into the East River   disrobe
and swim out to where I stand
white-knuckled to the deck rail
I hunger for the untarnished love
that lies beneath that flowing robe
but you must stand your guard
against complacency as I go out
to defend our common ground
Yet should I die on foreign soil
your beaming light
            will tell our story
                        to the world

Robert's Rules of Chaos

Rarely does a woman
      measure her entire life
Or even those years
      between 19 and 69
By the damage she's done
      to her male companions
Everything from her point
      of view has been
Right on the money
      and a perfect
Target for arrows she swiped
      from Cupid's quiver

Starlet's Pantoum Companion

A thinking woman never sleeps with monsters
unless perhaps her thoughts are misconstrued
like the starlet who was sure she'd win an Oscar
by playing parts where she is mostly nude

Unless perhaps her thoughts are misconstrued
like deadly sins served on a silver saucer
by playing parts where she is mostly nude
while knowing there are better things to offer

Like deadly sins served on a silver saucer
marring beauty   making her look crude
while knowing there are better things to offer
for well-endowed does not mean well-imbued

Marring beauty   making her look crude
it mainly frustrates those who want to sponsor
for well-endowed does not mean well-imbued
these are guidelines she'll be called to answer

It mainly frustrates those who want to sponsor
like the starlet who was sure she'd win an Oscar
these are guidelines she'll be called to answer
a thinking woman never sleeps with monsters

Dining Alfresco

Clumps of ripe elderberries bend down
offering kisses to cherry tomato vines
staked and arranged in wooden boxes

Marigolds around the brick patio form
a rectangle of stored-up light that refuses
to surrender to oncoming darkness

Long blond hair is another light source
and her out-stretched hands on the table
are desperately pale in comparison to his

The neighbor's dog won't stop barking
as though trying to scare the moon
pausing briefly with each passing cloud

They weren't really hungry so the turtle soup
with crackers and homemade elderberry
wine was sufficient to soak up any grief

He was pretty sure it'd been over for a while
but she didn't want to tell the children until
they set plans and made final decisions

The conservation was simple   They talked
about food   mostly in the past tense
occasionally mourning their loss of romance

They compared it to how the patio grew
dark whenever a cloud obscured the moon
a dimming neither of them could ignore

She had hoped in vain the wine might blend
their differences the way the moon softens
the patio with its palette of delicate colors

High overhead as if on autopilot an arrow
of geese head southward for no other reason
than a divine trust in their God-given instincts

Day Dreams

It's been days now   or maybe weeks
as I watch you come and go

It's when you're gone
that I fall in love with you again

Around you it's just infatuation
and here's how I know

Chaos cavorts in your shadow
I'm beginning to think she lives there

Don't get me wrong   it's not your fault
I fell in love with what you're not

I pretended you were or wanted you to be
that negative space in a Picasso

the white of an e. e. cummings poem
Of course I tended to fill in the blanks

and whenever we got together
I kept looking for what was missing

We both know the errors I make are made
in wanting more and wanting it now

But nothing will ever complete us
and nothing will completely destroy us

Always *The Phoenix*

When evil sweeps down like the pecking
of a great black bird   what frightens me most
is the flash and bang of it against a quiet
morning sun and how the afternoon of America
tastes of floating tar particles   pulverized quartz
and nothing moves as though we've become
the center of the universe   flags at half-mast
like wilting flowers on the cluttered nightstand
when you're sick   Our windows to the world
gain in importance when the rooms we occupy
are suddenly emptied and life itself turns
into a carnival ride we didn't pay for   jolting
surprising   shrieking   and finally ending
where it all began   We are all intruders here
chained to a relativistic fence Einstein didn't invent
Words to express this keep falling off the back
of the language wagon   The dead have joined
the crumpled titanium steel like what's left of canned
jelly in the cellar of a burned-out farmhouse
But reader take heed for as sure as sirens will cease
and bells will stop wailing *The Phoenix* shall rise again
and all across America a patched up Old Glory
will stand guard once more as another boiling pot
is pushed to the back burner to simmer and stew

Loneliness . . .

is heading downriver
again tonight
just like last night
and the night before
I see her from my bedroom
window
flowing white chiffon
negligee   glowing beneath
a smiling moon
as she paddles
her small two-seated
canoe

I imagine myself
filling the empty seat
playing my ukulele
and singing
Some say love
Is like a river
that drowns the tender reed

And if she wants
to go ashore
I'll beach the canoe
and offer her my hand
to disembark
We'll sit in the moonlight
side by side
on that flat rock
I'll continue my singing
Some say love
it is a hunger
an endless aching need

She'll begin a slow
sensual dance
along the riverbank
and won't bother to ask
my imagination to join her
he's here with me   glued
to my bedroom window

Unfinished . . .

It somehow seems cruel
that we are destined
to die
with unfinished . . .

I wonder if it was planned that way
by God
or by that tempestuous tempter
with horns   pitchfork
and treacherous . . .

Have an apple
     I'm not supposed to
You'll like it
     hmmmm
and so will . . .

and he did
for it brought her nakedness
to light
They feasted   together
and began to like that even . . .

You're outta here
     and take him with you
It was the Head Gardener speaking

but we're not finished

Finished with what

*the apple
and . . .*

It's Not About Us

Dumped from a box
like jig saw puzzle pieces
into a helpless heap

we learn to wait
for those interceding hands
that will sort us out

assemble us
turn us into that picture
we will never see

A for Anything

I'm Anything for Anybody
Any spirit   Any soul
Adding A to LGBTQ
has been a long-term goal

For if you're asked a preference
and don't know what to do
cause you've never felt you fit
in LGBT or Q

Then this can be your answer
it will make you want to sing
and maybe even feel some pride
in being Anything

I know we must be patient
but there will come the day
and all will be included
in LGBTQA

The Vaulted Sky

The great cathedral
of childhood
stands empty now
its vaulted ceiling of blue
a mere curio of the past
occasionally revisited
by the old man
who lives beneath
a vaulted sky so heavy
it requires the support
of myriad flying buttresses
erected solely
by his will to live

Dust

*—Genesis 3:19 for dust you are
and to dust you will return*

My mother used to say
    You are a handful
and she was right

for we are all
    handfuls of dust
dust that remembers

dust that sometimes clouds
    the pane between us
our mothers and the stars

dust that forgets
    dust that thinks it lives
dust that thinks it will die

but dust does not die
    dust is dust
and totally nothing but

Day of Reckoning

As a child when my mother scolded
I'd rebel even further and she'd say
There'll come a day of reckoning

Now that I'm older I dance my way out
bathe freely in a pious survival basin
and often walk the plank of indecision

My days can take on a rhythmic sway
like the mopping up of tracked-in water
and I forget how youth thrived on myth

So many things handcuff me to the past
bedeviling my desires to move forward
Memory skips like flat stones on water

Last night I took a midnight walk along
the insomniac seashore accompanied
by Grief who walks with a decided limp

He says my pile of fears will eventually
attain its angle of repose but I should
never blame blue skies for clouding over

None of this drivel is comforting to me
It simply stirs up that old desire to rebel
and so I let him know I'd rather be alone

An after-life of wildfire hugs the horizon
I let beach sand sift through my fingers
An echoing voice bounces off the waves

The day of reckoning is coming
          You'll be there
                    and she'll be there too

The Day Old Man Milnor Died

I stand in the wagon tracks
leading up to his faded red barn
across the street from our house
and watch the shiny black hearse
roll steadily up their long driveway
stopping short of the kitchen door
The day is all green   greener than
you'd think with bits of yellow dandelion
spread throughout   The weeds are high
and the hayloft mostly empty as is
the corn crib where blackbirds peck
like chickens hoping for a few kernels

Women from the Methodist Church
in wide-brimmed hats with veils are coming
by in droves with casserole dishes
paying their dues in comfort food and tears
I'm ten years old now yet feel the same way
I did five years ago when Papa died
but I won't get to see the body this time
and besides the stems on these dandelions
aren't long enough for a big bouquet

In a few weeks planting time will begin
and the old barn will be brought back to life
once again and by fall the bellies of both
the hayloft and corncrib will be full
What I'll miss the most about Mr. Milnor
will be knife sharpening time when he'll no
longer bring out their big set of butcher knives
and let me turn the crank on the grindstone
Sparks flew from every blade like shooting stars
the way it must have been when God made
the sun and moon on the 4th day   or maybe

more like on those first three days when God
himself was light   separated from darkness

Thanksgiving Eve

I named him Big Guy
kept him in our basement
in a wire cage
fed him shucked corn
three times a day
from the palm of my hand
and nights in my room
listened through the heating duct
to his gobbles and clucks

Big Guy was first prize
at the Cree Lake skeet shoot
last Saturday and my dad
happens to be the best shot
in Noble County

Now Big Guy's head
is out by the stump we used
as execution block
Mom's ironing the good white
tablecloth she only gets out
for special occasions
and I'm plucking at feathers
trying to sort out what it is
I'm supposed to be thankful for

Sugar Maple

I've been staring at you all day
by the wood's edge   waiting
and watching each numbered leaf
let go   There is no mourning
as your close-to-weightless
blood-red leaves flutter down
not as hummingbird wings
keeping a tiny life in balance
but as a rider-less raft on a river

My universe may well be parallel
to yours for the time will come
when I too must tip the waiter
for the wine of my last supper
and wait as the moon takes
one last sweep across my face
suggesting I release my grip
on all I've known since birth
and flutter to the forest floor

My Gift

It has been said
that when one spends time
with the dying
they leave you a gift
and I've been trying
to figure out
for over sixteen years
what yours was to me

I've adopted many
of your good habits
which have helped me
tremendously
but those are gifts
from a long life
together

I talk to you
through the yellow roses
that keep blooming
beneath my kitchen
window
but that bush was a gift
from your ladies' bridge club
which I planted
on the first anniversary
of your passing

It was only last night
that your gift
finally arrived
packaged neatly
around the frame
of our fifteen-year-old

granddaughter
whom you've never seen
as she came bounding in
from the patio
and for a brief moment
I thought you had come back

I'm in Tears

I hesitate to tell you I'm in tears
but you have left a void no one can fill
I know time heals but sometimes not for years

The sun has disappeared behind the hill
Clouds hover low as though foretelling rain
If you were here you'd take away the chill

And everything would feel so right again
I hope someday you'll have a change of mind
for chances are we both are feeling pain

When love gets lost it's very hard to find
though life goes on according to the spheres
and somehow gets us through the daily grind

until that day when love just reappears
I hesitate to tell you I'm in tears

Holly Leaf

Along its journey from tree to ground
a barbed holly leaf
impales itself upon the tip
of a Yucca spike

reminding me how as a child
I sat by the tracks secretly observing
trains   east and west   knowing I could
never cross over to the unwelcome side

All night my mind churns
like butter
as though mourning might bring me
a fresh loaf

When I wake from sleep I sweep away
the wadded-up napkins
green shards of wine bottles
and a few miscellaneous tears

Normally I'd be excited on moving day
but the two big stacks of boxes
one at each end of the living room
are marked *His* and *Hers*

and that image of two burley men
hoisting the tombstone into a cart
labeled   *Pleasant Acres*   won't fade
and like the holly leaf   I'm left

Facets of Love

I'm writing this   I suppose
because I miss our times together
Dinners followed by movies
or maybe dancing at Coral Gables
Canoe rides along the Red Cedar River
you with your ukulele   singing
Dry martini   jigger of gin
oh what a spell you've got me in
as I wield the wooden paddle
mostly working against the current
both of us a little high
Those were the days when neither
time nor money mattered
and one of love's facets was freedom
It's been more than a decade now
and I still haven't re-done the popcorn
ceiling in our bedroom   even though
I stare at it more frequently now
on nights when I lie awake   listening
to planes flying over the house
thinking you might surprise me with a visit
Freedom too   has its many facets
and heartache is only one of them
I'll be driving into town tomorrow
and rubbing eyeballs with reminders
of you strolling the wide sidewalks

War

I watch it run its course
from a distant bank

View its flashes and smoke
its smells cannot reach me

I Imagine the wretchedness
of instant piercings

Flinch as white phosphorous
scorches the open eyes of the dead

Burns the arms and legs
of comrades who muffle screams

I see muddy bomb craters
soaked with blood and tears

Picture the horror movies playing
daily in the minds of survivors

I shudder as barges line up
to unload the maimed and wounded

Wonder at the worth of it all
as I look up toward the heavens

The same heavens that shine
on the ill-founded furies of war

Euphemisms

By all reports it was a stray bullet
        but I say he was shot dead
                and I'll never get to see him again
Bullets don't stray like lost dogs
        or alley cats out scrounging
                for food or sexual pleasure
They're shot from guns
        and not like Puffed Wheat either
                straight out of a hollow steel barrel
Rifled ones are stabilized by spin
        but they're all affected to some extent
                by wind and gravity
In the case of long trajectories
        the Coriolis force even comes into play
                caused by Earth's rotation
I know I'm getting a bit technical here
        and maybe being a little blunt
                by saying outright that he was shot dead
rather than   he passed   or crossed over
        but I dearly loved him and won't see
                those fiery eyes of his again   ever
I guess the saving grace for you
        is that you didn't see him sprawled in the street
                blood oozing from his hoodie
and you didn't see him   stone cold   dead

The Dandelions Have Spoken

—Nature likes to hide itself—Heraclitus

I was five years old when my grandfather died
and beginning to lose the teachings of nature

but the tall dandelions that grew on the other side
of the gravel road had already told me about death

some taken young when housewives   like my mother
scoured the fields with paring knives in search of greens

those who survived blossomed into a million suns
reflecting their love in the faces of children

until they aged and went to seed   donned parachutes
and like my grandfather   sailed away in the wind

When Death Rings the Doorbell . . .

stands tall on my front steps
tapping one long narrow foot
like a door-to-door salesman
I won't ask him in nor will I
thank him for his information
When he leaves I'll be left alone
wondering why he's so callous
But maybe he doesn't like his job
dealing with people like me
or maybe he just doesn't care
and feels good he's escorted
another poor mortal into eternal life
where at this very moment a party
is developing to celebrate a new birth
Maybe I should get to know him better
after all he's said to be unavoidable
But I suspect when he comes for me
he won't be using the front door
Instead he'll jump me by surprise
and not even tell me what's happening
I'll be shoved kicking and screaming
into that surprise party waiting for me

Time

The unknown turning
into the known
to be remembered
or forgotten
and if forgotten
it doesn't exist
it may never have existed
Imagine if you and I
and everyone
were no longer able to remember
we would have
conquered time
The universe has been going on
like that forever
not knowing where it's been
or where it's going
Being is being
remembering being
is inventing time

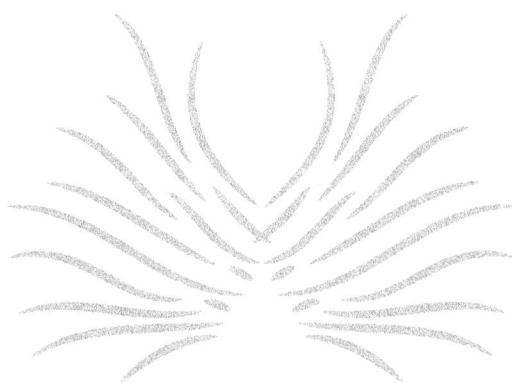

Acknowledgments

Thanks to Emilio Rizzo, proprietor and head barber of Cardiff by the Sea Barber Shop, shown on the cover, and to Randy Gieser posing as Chronos. Check out Randy's super Facebook page, Justclaus, for a little bit of Christmas any time of the year.

About the Author

R. T. Sedgwick is a poet living in Del Mar, CA. He has numerous published poems and his work appears in several anthologies. His first full length poetry book titled, "Left Unlatched" with sub-title, 'in hopes that you'll come in', 320 pp., published in 2011 by A Word with You Press, Oceanside, CA, was winner of the San Diego Book Awards prize for best poetry book published in 2011. In 2015 he published *The Sky is Not the Limit: and Other Select Poems.* Other poems and additional information can be found on his website, http://www. rtsedgwickpoems.com.

A Word with You Press

Editors and Advocates of Fine Stories in the Digital Age

A Word with you Press is a playful, passionate, and prolific consortium of writers, editors, designers and publishers who have been helping authors like yourself achieve their goals since 2009. We are drawn to the notion that nothing is more beautiful or powerful than a story well told. We help you tell it.

Writers and artists don't just happen; they are created by nurturing, mentoring, and by damn good editing. We provide this literacy triad through our interactive website, www.awordwithyoupress.com. Our regular writing contests give you an opportunity to hone your skills, and get both professional and peer feedback, as your entires are publsihed on the site and invite commentary.

We have helped first-time authors become award-winners, and we, ourselves, have won awards for writing, editing, and publishing excellence. The first step to writing your novel? Intent. If you've got it, let's talk. Send inquiries to Thornton Sully, at thorn@awordwithyoupress.com.

Thornton Sully has Jack-Londoned his way across the globe (most recently, Prague) sleeping with whatever country would have him, and picking up stray stories along the way. A litter of dog-eared passports that have taken up residence in his sock drawer are a constant temptation.

Bounce
by Pulitzer Prize winner Jonathan Freedman

A nutty watermelon man, a spurned she-lawyer, a frustrated carioca journalist and a misanthropic parrot set out to Brazil to change the world.

Raw Man
by Pulitzer-Prize nominee Fred Rivera, winner at the 2015 International Latino Book Awards

This lightly-novelized Vietnam memoir, now required reading at major universities, derives its title from the author's epiphany: "Twenty-seven years after I got on the flight home, I saw that Nam war was just raw man spelled backwards. I'm pretty raw today."

A Word with You, Vol. I
The Best from A Word with You Press

An anthology of select winners from the literary contests of *A Word with You Press* from 2009 to 2015

The Boy with a Torn Hat
by Thornton Sully

Debut novel was a finalist in the 2010 USA Book Awards for Literary Fiction

"Henry Miller meets Bob Dylan in this coming of age romp played out in the twisted alleyways and smoky beer halls of Heidelberg. Sully is a cunning wordsmith and master of bringing music to art and art to language. Excessive, expressive, lusty, and once in a blue metaphor—profound. Here is what I mean: 'Some women are imprisoned like a tongue in a bell—they swing violently but unnoticed until the moment of contact with the bronze perimeter

of their existence—and thenthe sound they make astonishes us its power and pain and beauty, and its immediacy' —Wunderbar"
—Jonathan Freedman, Pulitzer Prize winner

The Courtesans of God
by Thornton Sully
A novel based on the real life of a temple priestess
in the palace of the King of Malaysia.

Falling for France

by Nancy Milby

The first in *A Foreign Affair* series finds Annie Shaw
having to choose between a successful career and real
romance with a French aristocrat, and wanting both.

French Twist

by Nancy Milby

The saga continues as American archeologist Louise
Marcel becomes entangled in nasty business on French
soil, as she conceals her own hidden agenda.

Finding France

by Nancy Milby

The third in *A Foreign Affair* series finds Gabrielle Walker
lamenting a life unraveling when a letter informs her she is the
inheritor of a large estate in France. Then it gets complicated!

Finding Home

by Nancy Milby

Etienne, the recurring enigma in the series *A Foreign Affair*, is brutal to his enemies but a gentle giant to those he loves. Can the secret woman in his past enter his life again? Perhaps, but not with complications—some predictable, but some …

Visit our on-line store at www.awordwithyoupress.com. Most books are available as print editions and ebooks. We have also a growing selection of gifts for writers, and please check out our latest contests! We'd love a word from you!

A Word with You Press
Editors and Advocates of Fine Stories in the Digital Age
310 East A Street
Suite B
Moscow, Idaho 83843

Praise for Clipping the Wings of Chronos

"The speakers in Clipping the Wings of Chronos relish the moments that linger almost indefinitely if we will let them; they remind us that being is being / remembering being / is inventing time."

ADAM VINES, AUTHOR OF OUT OF SPEECH AND EDITOR OF BIRMINGHAM POETRY REVIEW

"This book is an unpretentious, honest, and beautifully uncertain exploration."

WESLEY ROTHMAN, TEACHING FELLOW AT THE CATHOLIC UNIVERSITY OF AMERICA

"This is a fine book of poetry, one I shall cherish because each poem makes you want to read it again, and to go on to the others that follow, with their range, depth and honesty of a man who observes well, feels life in and around him and who shares these important matters with others, unselfishly, as what a fine poet does… Carry on Robert."

PROFESSOR SAM HAMOD, PhD, THE IOWA WRITERS WORKSHOP, (RETIRED)

"Chronos, or time, in its merciless swiftness, steals everything as soon as we realize we have it, making incisions where it hurts most— taking away our loved ones, but the poet defeats time by insisting on beauty as the gift that survives."

SHADAB ZEEST HASHMI, AUTHOR OF AUTHOR OF GHAZAL COSMOPOLITAN, KOHL & CHALK, AND BAKER OF TARIFA